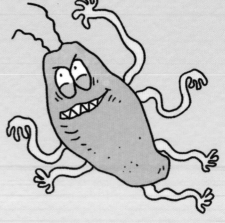

The Good Germ Hotel

Meet Your Body's Marvelous Microbes

By **Kim Sung-hwa** and **Kwon Su-jin**

Illustrated by **Kim Ryung-eon**

What on Earth Books

Oh, hello! You've arrived just at the right time. I'm on my way down to the ground floor. Would you like to join me?

I am a friendly gut bacterium, and I live inside a human being! She is a wonderful five-star hotel.

From your head to your toes, you are full of bacteria.

Bacteria are types of tiny living things called microbes. There are four common types of microbe. Some are bacteria, like me—lots of us are good, but some can cause infections. The other three common microbes are viruses, fungi, and protozoa. These all have good and bad versions too. A virus is a particle that can cause diseases, such as flu. Fungi are plant-like organisms that love damp places, such as sweaty feet. And some protozoa, called parasites, live inside and feed off other creatures.

But don't worry, I am one of the good bacteria, and I am here to help. This is a big day for me because I've decided to meet my hotel. Do you think she'll like me?

I am a good bacterium that lives in your gut. My suite is located on the middle floor, inside your intestines. I love it here. It's dark and cozy, and I get to eat lots of tasty food.

But what do you do in my body all day?

Well, I'm incredibly busy. I have lots of chores, such as helping to break down the food that you eat and sending the rest of your body the nutrients it needs. By the end of each day, I'm usually beat, but I love being a busy bacterium.

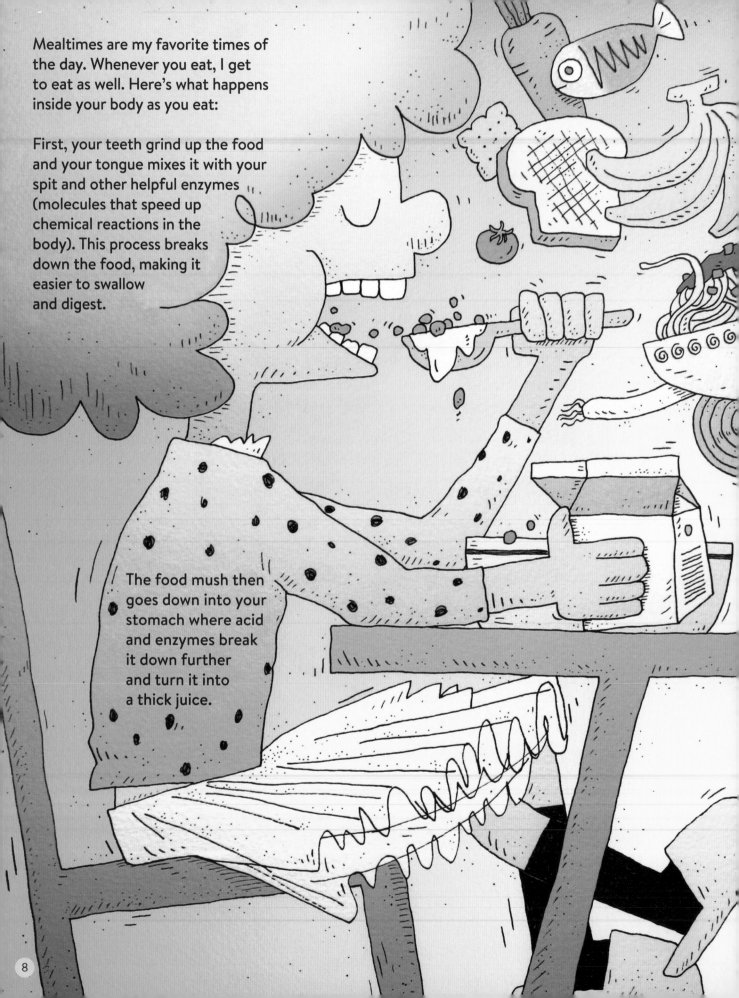

Mealtimes are my favorite times of the day. Whenever you eat, I get to eat as well. Here's what happens inside your body as you eat:

First, your teeth grind up the food and your tongue mixes it with your spit and other helpful enzymes (molecules that speed up chemical reactions in the body). This process breaks down the food, making it easier to swallow and digest.

The food mush then goes down into your stomach where acid and enzymes break it down further and turn it into a thick juice.

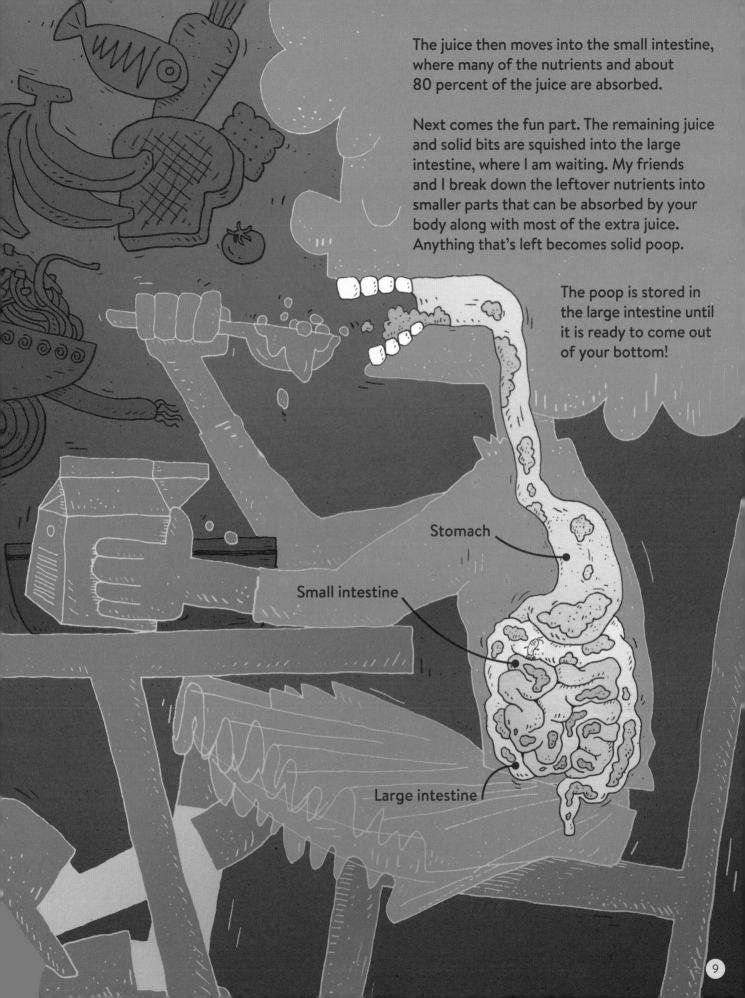

The juice then moves into the small intestine, where many of the nutrients and about 80 percent of the juice are absorbed.

Next comes the fun part. The remaining juice and solid bits are squished into the large intestine, where I am waiting. My friends and I break down the leftover nutrients into smaller parts that can be absorbed by your body along with most of the extra juice. Anything that's left becomes solid poop.

The poop is stored in the large intestine until it is ready to come out of your bottom!

Stomach

Small intestine

Large intestine

If you weigh 66 pounds (30 kilograms), you might have as many as 45 trillion good microbes living in and on your body.

That's so many!

Don't worry, we are peaceful and very, very tiny. We've lived in your hotel ever since you were a baby. I bet you never even noticed us!

I am the most famous of your gut bacteria.

My name is Colon *Bacteroides*.

VIP

People make a fuss about having us in their gut because they think we are the same as the bad bacteria or germs that make them sick. But most of us don't cause sickness. We live in your hotel and work hard to break down the food you eat. When our work is done, we leave your body in your poop.

Good microbes live on all floors of your hotel.

97

We live in your hair, skin, mouth, intestines, toes, and armpits, to name just a few of our favorite places.

You might be surprised by how much of your body weight is made up of good microbes.

Bacteria and other microbes can make up 3 percent of your body weight. So, if you weigh 66 pounds (30 kilograms), then about 2 pounds (1 kilogram) of that would be made up of good microbes.

I weigh about the same as a small pineapple.

64 lbs

+

2 lbs = 66 lbs

We microbes are super tiny, which means that you need a microscope to see us. But, even though we are small, we are mighty. There are more of us on Earth than all the animals combined.

Imagine a giant scale. Put all of the animals in the world on one side and all four types of microbes found on Earth on the other. What do you think would happen?

Hmm... I don't know!

Well, the scale would tilt toward microbes. Together we are heavier than all the animals! Impressive, huh?

Microbes can live anywhere. We can survive in deep oceans, frozen icebergs, boiling hot springs, or even in outer space! But I like living in your lovely hotel the best.

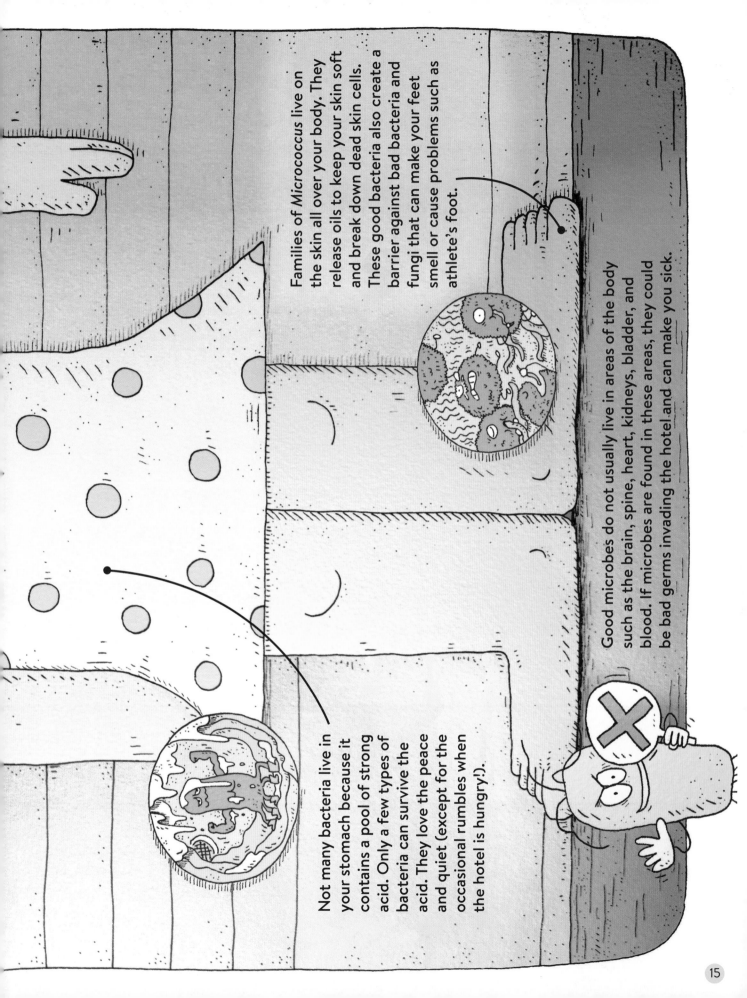

Families of *Micrococcus* live on the skin all over your body. They release oils to keep your skin soft and break down dead skin cells. These good bacteria also create a barrier against bad bacteria and fungi that can make your feet smell or cause problems such as athlete's foot.

Not many bacteria live in your stomach because it contains a pool of strong acid. Only a few types of bacteria can survive the acid. They love the peace and quiet (except for the occasional rumbles when the hotel is hungry!).

Good microbes do not usually live in areas of the body such as the brain, spine, heart, kidneys, bladder, and blood. If microbes are found in these areas, they could be bad germs invading the hotel and can make you sick.

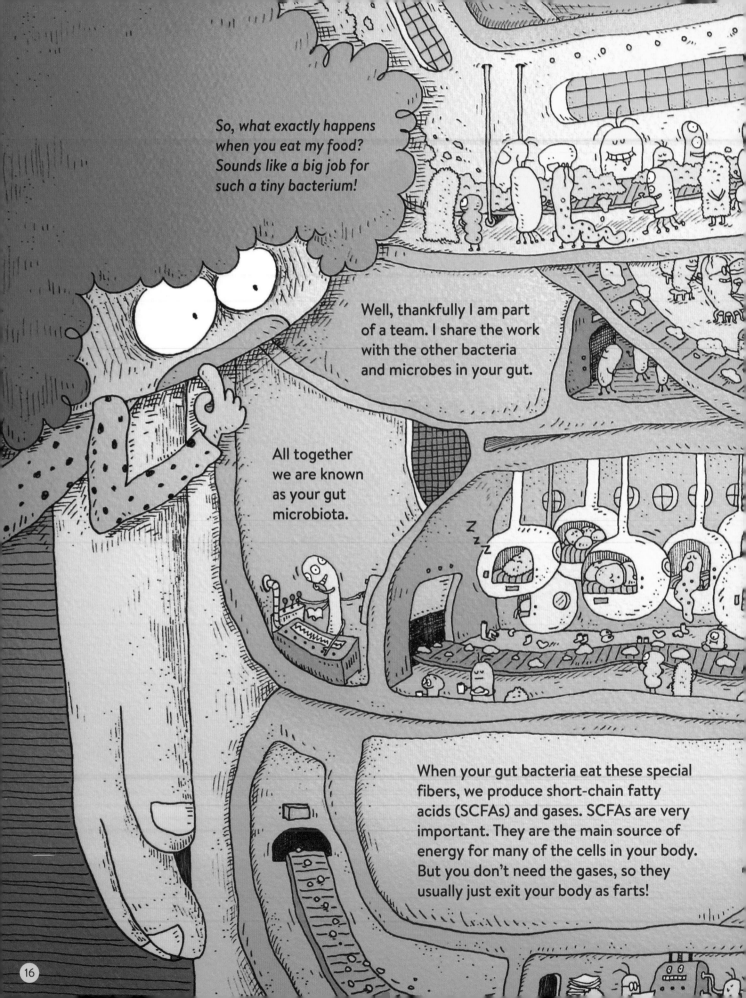

So, what exactly happens when you eat my food? Sounds like a big job for such a tiny bacterium!

Well, thankfully I am part of a team. I share the work with the other bacteria and microbes in your gut.

All together we are known as your gut microbiota.

When your gut bacteria eat these special fibers, we produce short-chain fatty acids (SCFAs) and gases. SCFAs are very important. They are the main source of energy for many of the cells in your body. But you don't need the gases, so they usually just exit your body as farts!

We all like to eat substances called prebiotics, which we get from your food. Prebiotics are types of dietary fiber that are found in many fruits and vegetables, such as onions, leeks, asparagus, watermelon, and bananas. They also help us to produce nutrients for the cells in the hotel's intestines. This leads to a healthier gut.

We are so good at our jobs that if good bacteria like us didn't exist, you would have to eat almost twice as much food to get the nutrients your body needs to work and grow.

Oh no, I would get too full!

Then I bet you're glad we are here!

Your intestines work kind of like a conveyor belt. The food passes through them and all the bacteria take turns removing the nutrients.

If it weren't for us, a lot of the important nutrients that your body needs would simply pass straight through and leave in your poop.

We are very professional and work day and night to keep the entire hotel running smoothly.

Protecting you from bad germs is also part of our job. One of the ways we do this is just by being here! When you're healthy, there are lots of us living in your intestines, so there is no room for bad germs to get in.

But, if the bad germs are really pushy, we can always call for backup. And we know just the cells for the job—your immune cells.

What are immune cells?

Immune cell

Immune cells are the hotel's army. The immune cell soldiers surround the invading germs and stick to them so that they can't escape. They can then fight and kill the invaders.

Immune cell

DANGER!

ALERT!

Every time the immune cell army meets a new invader, they try to memorize what it looks like and figure out its weak spots. That way, the immune cells can be ready with a battle plan to quickly locate and destroy the bad germs if they try to get in again.

If I have immune cells to fight bad germs, why do I get sick?

Well, it all depends on your body! In a healthy body, immune cells can usually kick bad germs out of the hotel.

And sometimes, you feel sick *because* your immune cells are doing their job. For example, in order to rid the hotel of invaders, your immune cells often have to fight fire with fire. They cause you to have a high temperature, or fever, to burn out the invaders. The bad germs can't stand the heat!

102°F

Sometimes a new germ, such as Covid-19, appears and your immune system might struggle to fight it. If the bad germ armies are stronger than your immune cells, you may get sick.

NAME: Strep throat (bacteria)
CAUSE: Breathing in sneeze or cough droplets from an infected person
SYMPTOMS: High fever, very sore throat with white patches, headache

But, when your immune cells are nice and strong and they recognize the invader, they are a great army. Their mission is to always stand their ground and defend your body from bad germs.

Hooray for immune cells!

NAME: Stomach bug (virus or bacteria)
CAUSE: Drinking or eating contaminated water or food or getting too close to an infected person
SYMPTOMS: Watery diarrhea, stomach pain or cramps, nausea, vomiting, and fever

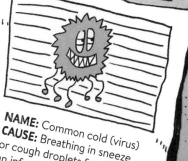

NAME: Common cold (virus)
CAUSE: Breathing in sneeze or cough droplets from an infected person
SYMPTOMS: Fever, headache, stuffy nose, sore throat, cough, body aches

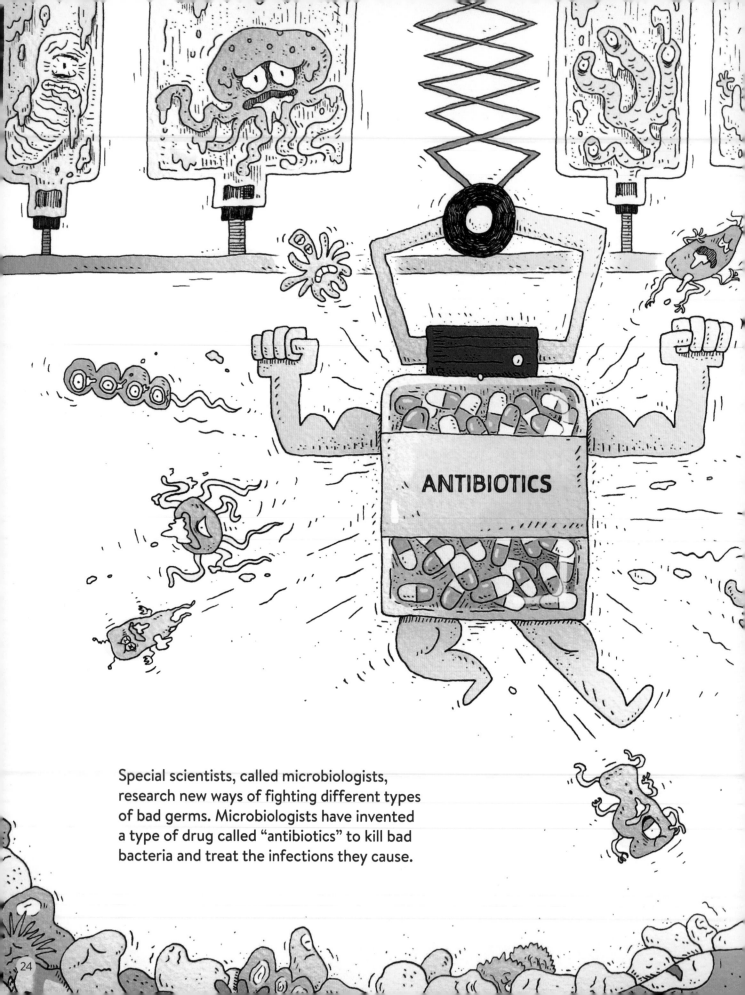

Special scientists, called microbiologists, research new ways of fighting different types of bad germs. Microbiologists have invented a type of drug called "antibiotics" to kill bad bacteria and treat the infections they cause.

Antibiotics are great—they save many lives. But there is a downside to this wonder-medicine.

Antibiotics can't tell the difference between bad bacteria and good bacteria like me! This means that in addition to killing invading bad bacteria, they kill good bacteria in the hotel, too.

PRESCRIPTION

If antibiotics kill off all the good bacteria in a hotel, it means that the human could get very sick. Without good bacteria, the hotel would not be able to defend itself against invaders!

Thankfully, scientists have learned that humans and bacteria need to work as a team. Doctors are learning not to give their patients antibiotics unless it's really necessary. That way we don't get harmed and can continue our work in the hotel. Hooray!

GERM-FREE ZONE

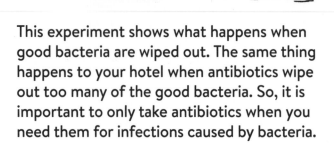

How do microbiologists study bacteria?

Well, they do experiments. Let me tell you about one particularly famous example.

This experiment shows what happens when good bacteria are wiped out. The same thing happens to your hotel when antibiotics wipe out too many of the good bacteria. So, it is important to only take antibiotics when you need them for infections caused by bacteria.

Once upon a time, there was a small white mouse that lived in a laboratory.

The scientists in the laboratory fed the mouse food without any good bacteria in it. They also kept the cage squeaky clean so that no bad bacteria could get in.

So, the mouse was all alone without any bacteria at all.

After one month, the scientists moved the mouse to a cage where other mice lived.

The other mice were full of good bacteria, and their cage had not been cleaned, so there was a small amount of bad bacteria in there too. The white mouse was nervous about moving to a new house.

And rightly so! The white mouse got sick very quickly in this new environment. It was not able to fight off bad bacteria because it had no good bacteria living in its body. And since it was not used to meeting bad bacteria, just a small amount of them made the white mouse really sick.

This experiment proved how important good bacteria are to living things. And how it's best to live in an environment with a little bit of dirt—and germs!

There is also another problem with using antibiotics. Some bad bacteria can learn how to resist antibiotics! And these bad bacteria survivors then reproduce to form whole armies of antibiotic-resistant bacteria. Yikes!

So, scientists had to make even stronger antibiotics. But the bad bacteria became resistant to those, too! And so scientists and bad bacteria are in a constant battle with one another. Who will triumph? We will have to wait and see...

I hope the scientists win!

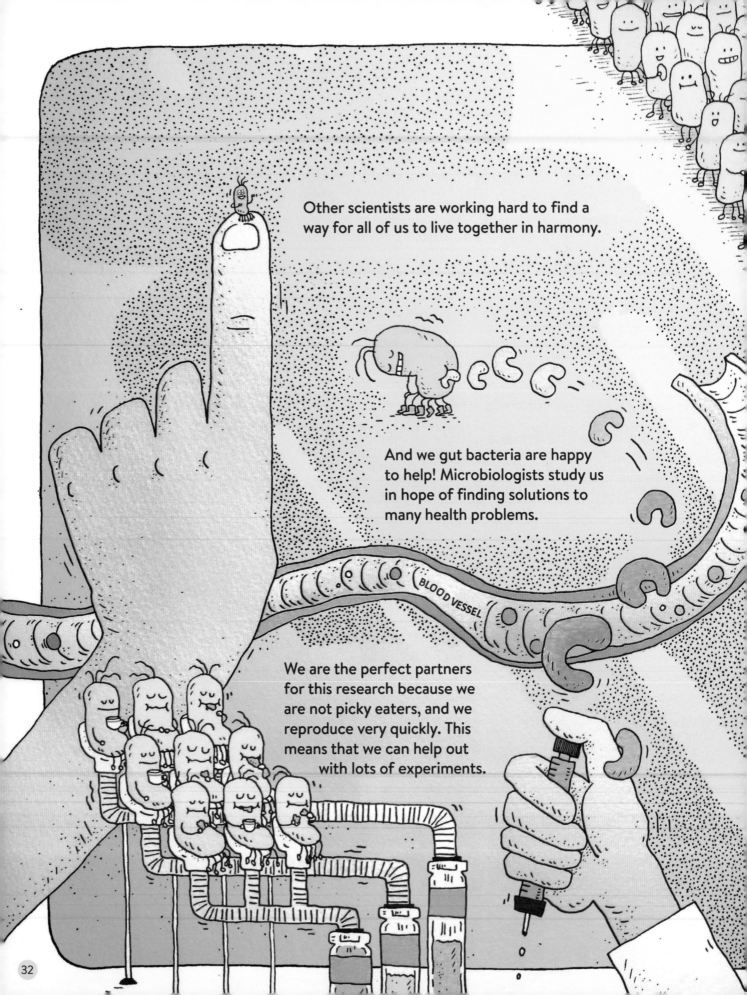

Other scientists are working hard to find a way for all of us to live together in harmony.

And we gut bacteria are happy to help! Microbiologists study us in hope of finding solutions to many health problems.

BLOOD VESSEL

We are the perfect partners for this research because we are not picky eaters, and we reproduce very quickly. This means that we can help out with lots of experiments.

My army of gut bacteria are teaching scientists all about how we fight off infections all over the body, even in the brain and heart.

We've been doing such a good job that some scientists have won prizes for all of our hard work! But stay tuned because our work has only just begun!

Some people have started to recognize just how important good bacteria are. They buy foods and pills called probiotics from the store. These are wonderful because they add to the good bacteria in their hotel. Other people even feed us the prebiotics we like to eat to keep us happy.

In the future, we would love it if more people helped keep us healthy. Maybe humans will use good-bacteria soaps or put good bacteria shoe inserts inside sneakers to stop them from smelling bad! I hope this all happens soon. Then we would be much better at doing our jobs.

Well, I think you're fantastic. Thank you for keeping me healthy and happy!

You're welcome! We're very happy to have finally met you. You can now count us all as your friends.

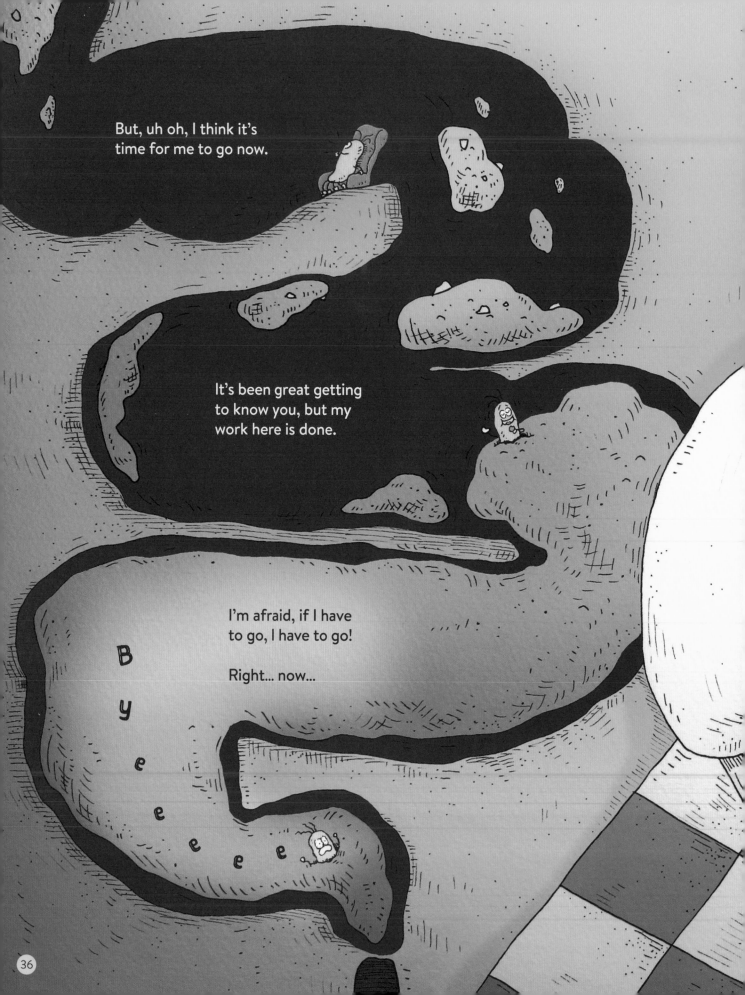

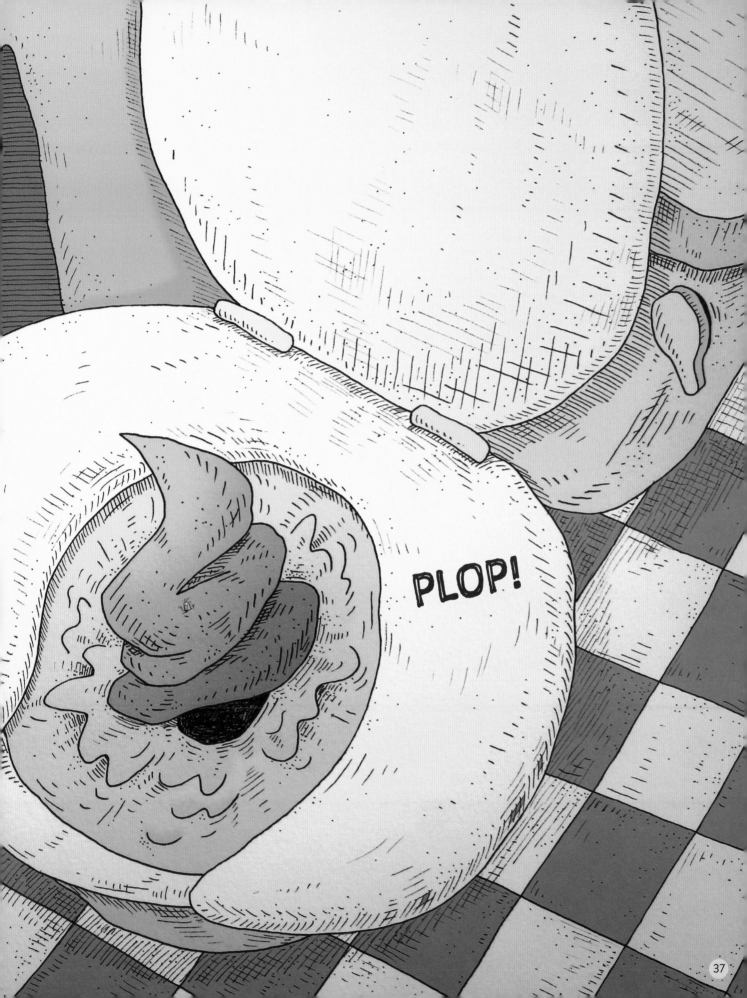

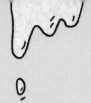

Glossary

antibiotics
A type of medicine that kills bacteria.

athlete's foot
A type of infection caused by a fungus that is usually found between a human's toes. It results from too much sweat or tight-fitting shoes.

bacteria
The plural form of the word bacterium.

bacterium
A type of single-celled, tiny life form.

cell
A basic structure, or building block, from which all living things are made.

contaminated
Something that has become impure or dirty by coming into contact with a polluted substance.

diarrhea
Watery poop. A person that has diarrhea often needs to poop more than usual. It can be caused by many different illnesses.

enzyme
A protein produced by a living organism that speeds up chemical reactions in that organism.

fungi
The plural form of the word fungus.

fungus
An organism, such as a mold, yeast, or mushroom that feeds on organic matter.

germ
Microorganisms that can be bacteria, fungi, viruses, or protozoa.

gut
The digestive system. It includes the mouth, esophagus, stomach, pancreas, liver, gallbladder, intestines, colon, and rectum.

gut microbiota
All of the microbes (bacteria, fungi, protozoa, and viruses) that live within a human gut.

infection
What happens when a foreign organism enters the body and causes disease.

intestines
The lower part of the gut, located between the stomach and the anus.

laboratory
A place where scientists conduct experiments.

microbe
A microorganism, such as a bacterium.

microbiologist
A type of scientist who studies microscopic life forms.

microorganism
A very tiny, simple life form, for example a bacterium, virus, fungus, or protozoa.

microscope
A device that is used to see tiny things that are too small to be seen by the naked eye.

molecule
The smallest unit of substance, formed by two or more atoms joined together.

nausea
A feeling of sickness with an urge to throw up.

nutrients
Substances in food that are needed for life and growth. Some examples are proteins, vitamins, and minerals.

organism
Any living thing, from a single-celled life form to an individual animal or plant.

parasite
An organism that lives on or in another organism, known as a host, and gets its food from that host.

prebiotic
A food ingredient that promotes the growth of good microorganisms in your gut.

probiotics
Microorganisms, such as bacteria and yeast, that are found in some foods or taken as pills. They are thought to have many health benefits, such as helping to keep the natural balance of good bacteria in the gut.

protozoa
Single-celled organisms that live in a wide variety of moist habitats including freshwater, saltwater, and soil.

reproduce
To multiply.

virus
A microbe that may cause disease in people, animals, and plants. Viruses cause many diseases, including colds, flu, and Covid-19. Smaller than bacteria, viruses reproduce by getting inside living cells and making copies of themselves to spread throughout the body.

Index

Selected Sources

Arnold, Nick (2014). *Disgusting Digestion (Horrible Science)*. Scholastic.

Bacteria Give Feet 4 Distinct Odors https://discovermagazine.com/planet-earth/bacteria-give-feet-4-distinct-odors

Blech, Jörg (2001). *Mensch & Co.* Rowohlt Tb.

Can Gut Bacteria Improve Your Health? https://www.health.harvard.edu/staying-healthy/can-gut-bacteria-improve-your-health

Enders, Giulia (2017). *Darm mit Charme: Alles über ein unterschätztes Organ.* Ullstein Verlag GmbH.

Herrick, John (2004). *Les Bactéries sont-elles nos ennemies?* Pommier.

How a Well Adapted Immune System Remembers https://www.pnas.org

Knight, Rob and Buhler, Brendan (2015). *Follow Your Gut: How the Ecosystem in Your Gut Determines Your Health, Mood, and More: The Enormous Impact of Tiny Microbes.* Simon & Schuster, Ted Books.

Kornberg, Arthur (2008). *Germ Stories.* University Science Books, U.S.

Lee Jeong-mo (2012). *I Am the Super Microorganism.* Woongjin Thinkbig.

https://www.monash.edu/medicine/ccs/gastroenterology/home

Protection Against Pathogens https://www.umassmed.edu/microbiome/junk-pages/protection-against-pathogens/

Sakamoto, Shiho and Tara, Mimiro (2016). *Unchi No Shoutai Kin Wa Jinrui Wo Sukuu.* Miseghy.

What on Earth Books is an imprint of What on Earth Publishing
Allington Castle, Maidstone, Kent ME16 0NB, United Kingdom
30 Ridge Road Unit B, Greenbelt, Maryland, 20770, United States

First published in English in 2021 by What on Earth Books
Translation copyright © 2021 What on Earth Books
Copyright © 2017 Woongjin Thinkbig
Text by Kim Sung-hwa and Kwon Su-jin
Illustrations by Kim Ryung-eon
World English translation rights arranged with Woongjin Thinkbig Co, Ltd. on
behalf of S.B. Rights Agency—Stephanie Barrouillet

Staff for this book:
Editor, Katy Lennon
Designer, Daisy Symes

Consultants: Chun Jong-sik and Dr. Laurie Duncan

Library of Congress Cataloging-in-Publication Data available upon request

ISBN: 978-1-9137501-6-9

Printed in China

10 9 8 7 6 5 4 3 2 1